Emergency Workers

Phillip Simpson

Emergency Workers

Text: Phillip Simpson
Publishers: Tania Mazzeo and Eliza Webb
Series consultant: Amanda Sutera
   Hands on Heads Consulting
Editor: Gemma Smith
Project editor: Annabel Smith
Designer: Leigh Ashforth
Project designer: Danielle Maccarone
Permissions researcher: Catherine Kerstjens
Production controller: Renee Tome

Acknowledgements
We would like to thank the following for permission to reproduce
copyright material:

Front cover: Shutterstock.com/Jaromir Chalabala; p. 1, 12: iStock.
com/GummyBone; p. 3, 15: Shutterstock/Phil Whitten; p. 4: iStock.
com/Burak Sür; p. 5 (top): Shutterstock.com/Take Photo, (bottom): Getty
Images/Eddie Safarik/AFP; p. 6: Alamy Stock Photo/Guy Bell; p. 7 (top left):
Shutterstock.com/Art Konovalov, (top right): Shutterstock.com/Stock Unit,
(bottom left): iStock.com/Butsaya, (bottom right): ESTA – Gavin Blue; p. 8:
Alamy Stock Photo/Steve Turner; p. 9 (top): iStock.com/lovleah, (bottom):
Shutterstock.com/www.hollandfoto.net; p. 10: iStock.com/gorodenkoff; p.
11 (top): Newspix/Rohan Kelly, (bottom): Alamy Stock Photo/Diarmuid
Curran; p. 12 (bottom): Shutterstock.com/Jeff Thrower; p. 13 (top): AAP
Image/Hualien City Government, (bottom): Alamy Stock Photo/Nancy G
Fire Photography, Nancy Greifenhagen; p. 14 (top), 20 (bottom): iStock.
com/Tashi-Delek, (bottom): iStock.com/Julia Gomina; p. 15 (top):
Shutterstock.com/Phil Whitten, (bottom): Shutterstock.com/Gorodenkoff;
p. 16 Shutterstock.com/Monkey Business Images; p. 17 (top): iStock.
com/SDI Productions, (bottom): 123RF.com/jk21; pp. 18, 20, 21: ESTA –
Gavin Blue; p. 19: Shutterstock.com/pixelaway; p. 22 (left): Alamy Stock
Photo/Robert Convery, (right), back cover (middle): Shutterstock.
com/sirtravelalot; p. 23 (top), back cover (right): iStock.
com/monkeybusinessimages, (bottom left), back cover (left): iStock.
com/kali9, (bottom right): Shutterstock.com/Ka Iki.

Every effort has been made to trace and acknowledge copyright.
However, if any infringement has occurred, the publishers tender their
apologies and invite the copyright holders to contact them.

Special thanks to Amber Webb and ESTA for their assistance with this
book.

NovaStar

Text © 2024 Cengage Learning Australia Pty Limited

ISBN 978 0 17 033407 5

Cengage Learning Australia
Level 5, 80 Dorcas Street
Southbank VIC 3006 Australia
Phone: 1300 790 853
Email: aust.nelsonprimary@cengage.com

For learning solutions, visit **cengage.com.au**

Printed in China by 1010 Printing International Ltd
1 2 3 4 5 6 7 28 27 26 25 24

*Nelson acknowledges the Traditional Owners and Custodians
of the lands of all First Nations Peoples. We pay respect
to Elders past and present, and extend that respect to
all First Nations Peoples today.*

Contents

Emergencies   4

Emergency Workers   6

  Police Officers   8

  Firefighters   10

  Paramedics   14

  Emergency Care Nurses and Doctors   16

  Emergency Call-Takers   18

Meet an Emergency Worker   20

An Important Role   22

Glossary and Index   24

Emergencies

An emergency is when something happens to put a person's life, health or **property** in danger.

Some emergencies are life-threatening. This means that a person may die if they don't get help quickly – for example, if they are having a **heart attack**.

This person needs an oxygen mask to help him breathe.

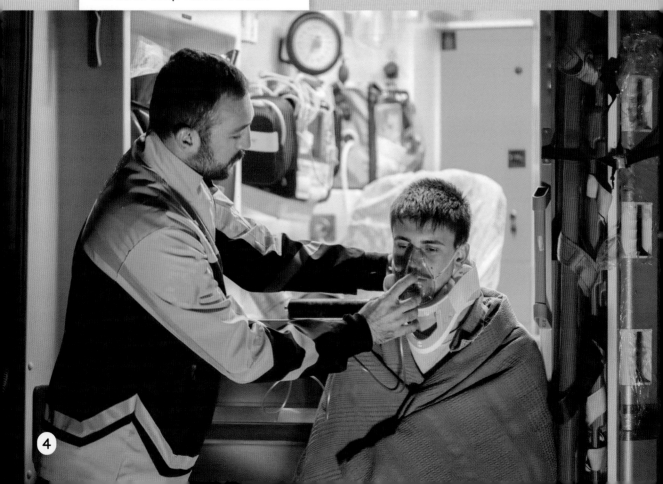

An emergency can also be when someone is hurt or trapped, or when a building is badly damaged.

Natural disasters, such as floods and bushfires, are also emergencies, because they can be a danger to human life.

Storms can blow trees into buildings.

These people are being rescued from a flooded street.

Emergency Workers

So, who helps us in an emergency?
These people are called emergency workers.

Police officers, firefighters and **paramedics** are emergency workers. There are other types of emergency workers, too, such as emergency care nurses and doctors, and emergency call-takers.

This police officer is directing traffic away from an accident.

firefighter

paramedic

emergency care nurses and doctors

emergency call-taker

It can take years of training to become an emergency worker. These people must know how to act quickly to save lives and protect others.

Police Officers

The job of a police officer is to try to protect people's lives and property. Police officers are often called to help out in an emergency. Sometimes, they need to keep people away from the area around an emergency. For example, the police might close the roads around a flood.

Police officers stop people from driving through dangerous floodwater.

Police officers might also call for help from other emergency workers. For example, if there has been an accident and people are hurt, the police will call for a paramedic.

Police officers and firefighters work together in an emergency.

Police help paramedics at an accident.

Firefighters

Firefighters are emergency workers who take action when there is a fire. They are trained to put out different kinds of fires, such as fires in buildings and bushfires.

Firefighters use special equipment, such as fire trucks with ladders, hoses and tanks loaded with water.

A firefighter carries a person away from a fire.

This dog has been rescued from a bushfire.

A plane drops water onto flames.

For some large fires, **aerial** firefighters use special helicopters or planes. The helicopters and planes can pick up water from nearby rivers, dams or lakes. The plane then flies low to the ground to drop the water onto the fire.

Firefighters are sometimes called to help at bad car accidents. This is because a car can catch fire after a crash.

Lights and sirens on the fire truck warn people to move out of the way.

Firefighters also have equipment like **mechanical claws** that can pull open damaged vehicles to free trapped people. The claws are also known as the "jaws of life".

Mechanical claws can cut through a car door.

Firefighters use their equipment to rescue people who become trapped under **rubble** after disasters such as earthquakes.

Firefighters rescue somebody from a fallen building after an earthquake.

Firefighters also talk to people in the community about fire safety.

Firefighters help to keep the community safe day and night.

Paramedics

Emergency workers who help people who need **medical care** straight away are called paramedics.

Paramedics go to an emergency in an ambulance. When they arrive, they quickly work out what is wrong with the sick or **injured** person.

A paramedic helps a woman who is having trouble breathing.

An ambulance rushes to an emergency.

If the **patient** needs to go to hospital, the
paramedic gives them medical care first.
The patient is then taken
to hospital in an ambulance,
or in a helicopter called an
air ambulance.

The paramedic cares for the
patient in the ambulance
on the way to hospital.

Often, the quickest way to get
to hospital is by air ambulance.

A paramedic checks her patient's
heartbeat and breathing.

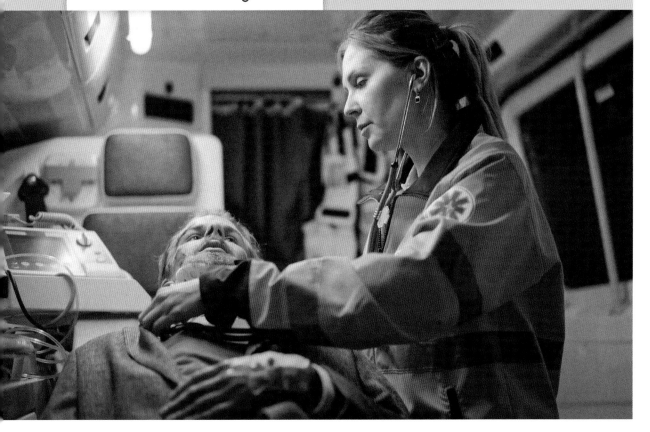

Emergency Care Nurses and Doctors

Nurses and doctors are emergency workers who are trained to help when a patient arrives at hospital.

An emergency care nurse will quickly work out how sick or injured a patient is. If the patient's injury or illness is life-threatening – for example, if they need an operation – then they will be treated by a doctor.

Emergency care nurses and doctors work together to help a patient.

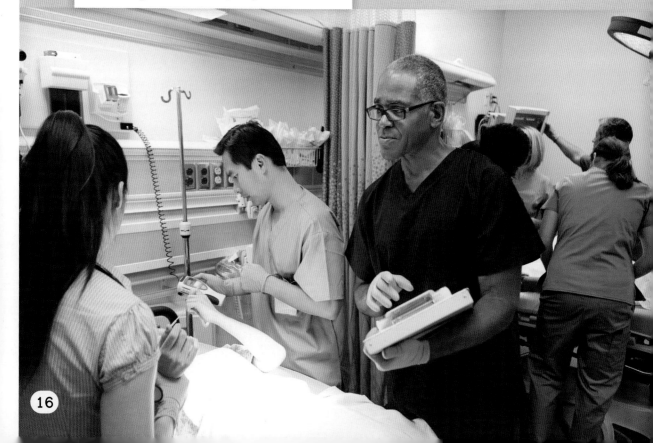

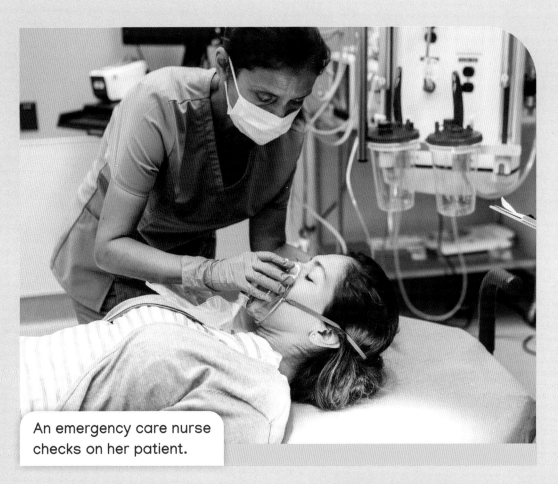

An emergency care nurse checks on her patient.

Emergency care nurses and doctors make sure they help the sickest or most badly injured patients first.

If a patient's illness or injury is not life-threatening, such as a broken arm, they might be sent for some tests. They may also need an **x-ray**.

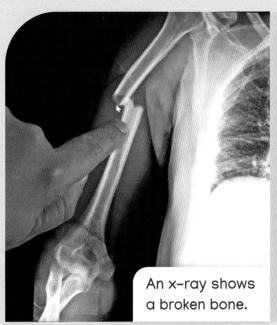

An x-ray shows a broken bone.

Emergency Call-Takers

An emergency call-taker is someone who answers phone calls from people who need help from the police, firefighters or paramedics.

An emergency call–taker listens to the caller as they explain the emergency.

The caller gets advice from the emergency call–taker.

The emergency call-taker gathers information from the caller about what has happened and where the emergency is. They also give instructions to the caller on what to do before help arrives.

Call-takers are trained to listen carefully and to speak clearly. They help the person on the phone to stay calm.

Meet an
Emergency
Worker

"My name is Amber. I work as an ambulance call-taker. My job is to answer calls from people who call the emergency phone number.

When a person makes an emergency call, they say if they need the police, firefighters or paramedics.

My job is to find out exactly what has happened and the address of the emergency. I can then send help.

Sometimes, I stay on the phone with the caller and give them care and advice until help arrives.

I wear a **telephone headset** so that I can use my hands to type the information into my computer.

The best thing about my job is helping people who might be having a really bad day. The hardest part is hearing from people who are upset or hurt. But most of the time, I love my job, because I like helping people. 🟨

An Important Role

Emergency workers make decisions every day, in many different emergencies. They must be ready to act quickly at any time. Most of all, they must want to help other people and to keep them safe.

Emergency workers play an important role in our communities. Without them, who would help us when we are sick, injured or in danger?

police officer

firefighters

emergency care nurses and doctors

paramedic

DID YOU KNOW?

Emergency phone numbers are different around the world. In Australia, the emergency phone number is triple zero, or 000.

Glossary

aerial (*adjective*)	something that happens up in the air
heart attack (*noun*)	a medical problem when blood can't flow to the heart properly
injured (*adjective*)	hurt or damaged
mechanical claws (*noun*)	machine hands that can grab, move and break things open
medical care (*noun*)	looked after by a doctor or nurse
paramedic (*noun*)	a person trained to give emergency help to injured or sick people before they get to hospital
patient (*noun*)	a person who is being given care or treatment by a doctor or nurse
property (*noun*)	something belonging to someone, e.g. a house, TV or car
rubble (*noun*)	broken-up bits of stone and waste, often from a building
telephone headset (*noun*)	headphones with a microphone attached that can be used to hear and talk to someone, without needing to hold a telephone
x-ray (*noun*)	a picture of inside the body

Index

accidents   6, 9, 12

ambulance/air ambulance   14, 15, 20

call-takers   6, 7, 18–19, 20–21

disasters   5, 13

doctors   6, 7, 16–17, 23

emergency call   18–19, 20–21

fires   5, 10, 11, 12, 13

firefighters   6, 7, 9, 10–13, 18, 20, 22

floods   5, 8

heart attack   4, 24

injury   14, 16, 17, 22

medical care   14, 15, 24

nurses   6, 7, 16–17, 23

paramedics   6, 7, 9, 14–15, 18, 23, 24

police officers   6, 8–9, 18, 20, 22